Overnight Accuracy

How To Improve Your Shooting Accuracy In One Evening

US Concealed Carry Association

www.USConcealedCarry.com

U.S. CONCEALED CARRY AND CONCEALED CARRY MAGAZINE DISCLAIMER

AUTHOR'S DISCLAIMER

Contents

Introduction: Prepare to be BLOWN AWAY.

reetings fellow armed citizen! My name is Patrick Kilchermann, and I'm proud to be a team member of the United States Concealed Carry Association.

The Best You're Going To Find.

Our motto at the United States Concealed Carry Association is that we are the Ultimate Resource for the Armed Citizen. Everything we do is measured against this motto. It's common for owner and founder Tim Schmidt to ask me "Is this video tip that we're about to email our members representative of what you'd expect from the Ultimate Resource for the Armed Citizen?" If so, we run it. If not- we cut it.

Deadly Accuracy.

What makes us the Ultimate Resource for the Armed Citizen? First, we give the best information, because we only give information that is the proven truth. Not everyone can say that, but some can. So, we take it one step further: We are committed to giving you the BEST information in the fastest, most easily absorbed manner. For example, all of our special reports and books include audio versions for mp3 players, or for your car CD player- not everyone learns by reading!

Perhaps most importantly, our information gets straight to the point. You are about to learn how to improve your handgun accuracy overnight. In reality, you'll learn how to do this in about fifteen minutes, but we thought that might seem unbelievable. Trust me- it's not. Here's the USCCA difference:

Handgun Accuracy is EASY.

The reason other handgun accuracy instructional books, videos, and articles take so long to get through, is because they are filled with fluff. Their authors don't want to leave you feeling short-changed. This is the 'paid by the hour' mentality. At the USCCA, we are totally results oriented. We don't tolerate fluff, and neither should you. If there is one thing you will never find in any of our publications, it's filler and fluff- whether it's our flagship *Concealed Carry Magazine*, or *How to Detect Lies and Liars*, or *How to Transform Fear Into a Powerful Ally*, or *The Ultimate Buggin' Out and Stayin' Alive Crash Course*, or the report that this guide was derived from, *107+ Handgun Accuracy Secrets*.

The reason is this: Being an effectively armed and prepared citizen is NOT hard. You don't need to study at a university for four years to master it, and you don't need to devote a week to a 400-page book on the subject.

The Ultimate Warrior.

Sure, we can always get better. We can always improve our skills in handgun accuracy, for example. But what we found is this: While it may take thousands of rounds of practice to get your groups at 25 yards from four inches to two inches…. It takes ZERO shots to get your groups at 25 yards from twenty four inches (or worse) to six inches.

And while it may take years of training to be able to effectively combat multiple threats from a sitting position with your carry-gun, it only takes a few solid principals to make sure that, if some sicko jumps you in an alley, YOU are going to be the one going home at night.

We wanted the SECRETS of shooting well.

In 2007, we recognized that while there was a TON of material available on shooting, there was nothing in the way of a 'be all, end all' accuracy guide that could be read and understood in a day.

Sure, there were volumes on the subject, but it's really not that difficult. The most experienced shooters will tell you that the biggest problem new shooters have, is that they over complicate things. Well, it's no wonder they do, when they see 300 page books devoted to gripping your handgun.

We wanted to change all that, and offer people something that could be entirely digested in an afternoon or evening, which would tell them the secrets of handgun accuracy. We wanted people to be able to become noticeably better after just one night, and give them the tools and knowledge that would allow them to master their handguns through cheap practice (that doesn't involve shooting up all your ammo stock).

We had no idea how simple it would be.

The product of our searching was a 51 page book titled '107+ Handgun Accuracy Secrets'. Seven world-famous marksmen and trainers contributed to make it happen, and we proudly offer this book as one of our highest achievements. It's truly a masterpiece, and it contains everything that one must know to truly master his or her handgun.

What you are about to read is a report on a few of these key secrets- and I personally guarantee you that this report will boost your accuracy overnight.

Stay safe,

Patrick Kilchermann

Section 1: The One and Only True Secret to Handgun Accuracy.

If you were to clamp your handgun into a vice and fire it at a target from ten yards, what do you think would happen? I'll tell you what would happen, and it doesn't matter if you're shooting a Kimber 1911, a GLOCK, or a Baretta Bobcat .22LR. What would happen is this: your handgun would fire nearly perfect groups.

Why then, do you suppose that when you take the same gun into your hands, your groups are nowhere near perfect? It's simple- your gun is not pointing where you want it to hit. It may seem like it is, but you must realize that it takes very little movement to throw off the point of impact.

Consider this: Your barrel is a straight line, and at ten yards, your bullet exits the barrel and is flying in a near-perfect straight path. Let's say that your barrel is four inches long. That means that over ten yards, your bullet must travel 90 barrel-lengths in free flight before it hits the target.

Using simply trigonometry, we know that by moving the tip of your barrel just ONE DEGREE to the left or right will make your bullet hit 6.3 inches to the left or right over just TEN yards. And that is just ONE degree. Many 'flinches' exhibited by shooters cause a shift of 3 degrees or more.

Here's another experiment. Take a laser-pointer, and stand ten yards from a target. Without turning the laser on, hold it as solid as you can, pointing straight at your bullseye. This should feel easy. You may notice it moving a tiny bit, but it's otherwise solid. Now turn the laser on. You'll see it dancing all around the bullseye- within a 1-2 inch circle if you're very solid, but more if you're not. Now try moving your pointer (trigger) finger around, and watch it really dance.

So let me sum this up. Pay attention, because everything that you are about to read and learn is based on this premise: IF you are not cutting perfect holes at 10 yards with your handgun, THEN you are moving your gun away from the point of aim before the bullet leaves the barrel.

The beauty of this 'if/then' statement is that it boils handgun accuracy (at any range) down to one simple fact: Improving your accuracy is as simple as holding your handgun steadier.

Here is how we're going to use this fact to teach you to achieve better accuracy overnight, and deadly accuracy over time:

First, we're going to talk about the correct way to grip a handgun.

Second, we'll talk about trigger control and flinching.

Third, we'll talk about how you can practice these secrets to boost your accuracy by a factor of four or higher. Remember that this is going to work as well for one handed shooting, weak handed shooting, shooting at extremely long ranges, and shooting while moving around.

■

Section 2: Grip--The Maker or Breaker of Handgun Accuracy.

The foundation of all handgun accuracy lies within your grip on the gun itself. With a solid enough grip, it really doesn't matter if you flinch, or perform a less than perfect trigger press. Granted, we will never have a truly rock-solid grip, so these other factors are important. It is important to know though, that in this and all other senses, your grip is the key to handgun accuracy.

The first thing we need to establish is the proper grip form.

Remember to grip as high as possible on the gun's handle. Your "strong hand" (the hand with your trigger finger) should contact the entire back edge of the handle, and the webbing between your thumb and index finger should make solid contact with the 'dovetail' of the back of the handle (if there is one).

Most handguns have this dovetail, as it protects your hand from being damaged by the slide on an automatic, or from interfering with the hammer on a standard revolver. The higher you grip, the more in-line with the barrel your hand will be, which will give you a HUGE advantage in accuracy by reducing the recoil and recovery time needed between shots . Remember that the lower you grip, the more the pistol will twist in your hand from the shot's recoil, and the less accurate, and the slower you will be. **Grip high**.

For a one-handed grip, the gun should slant at a 45 degree angle inward, so that the slide is closer to your chest, and the handle points toward your back. If this doesn't make sense, try this: Turn your head to your right (if you're right handed), and point with your index finger at eye level, as if someone just asked you where the cups are. Your hand should be relaxed, and the rest of your fingers should curve naturally into a very loose fist. Notice how your hand is not straight up and down, but instead is on a slant. Your index finger is almost like the peak of a roof, and the top and side of your hand are like uneven roof pitches. This is the natural way that your hand will point, and so it is very important to maintain this natural slant when gripping with one hand.

For a two handed grip, the gun should be held perfectly vertical. Grip with your strong hand as tightly as you would grip a hammer to drive a nail. Take note of the way your hand looks on the gun. Your finger should curl around the handle. On a small gun, your fingers may wrap completely around the handle and touch your palm. On a larger gun, they may stop half-way around the handle. It really doesn't matter, just take note of the way they look. Make sure your hand is in solid contact with the dove-tail (if there is one) and also make sure that your middle finger is in contact with the bottom of the trigger guard. Your thumb will most likely curve down and naturally touch the end of your middle finger.

Now, bring your "weak hand" (non-trigger finger hand) into the picture. Your weak hand should conform perfectly to your strong hand in the following ways:

Palms/Wrist: Your palms should touch at their base- not directly behind the handle, but at the side of the back edge of it, so that if you were to shoot, the gun would be pushed straight into the base of the palm on your strong hand.

Fingers: All four of your weak-hand fingers should lie on top of your three strong hand fingers (which are gripping the handle below the trigger guard). These four weak-hand fingers should fit nicely into the groves formed between the three strong-hand fingers, and your weak-hand pinkie will fall below your strong-hand pinkie. If your handle is long enough, the weak-hand pinkie may contact the handle, or in the case of a small gun, it may cup beneath the handle. Depending on the gun, your weak-hand fingers may not wind up in the grooves of the strong-hand fingers, but may in fact lie directly over them. Either way is acceptable- the goal is stability.

Thumbs: The palm bases should contact each other all the way up the side of the gun's handle, but you MAY have to lift the thumb of your strong hand slightly in order to accommodate the weak-hand's thumb. The weak-hand's thumb will start almost where the strong-hand's thumb ends, and I like to gently press my weak-hand thumb against the frame of the handgun for added stability. (Note! If you're shooting a revolver, make sure that your weak-hand thumb is BEHIND the cylinder. A LOT of gas and pressure escapes just forward of the cylinder, and it can burn you.)

The second thing we need to establish is grip-strength.

Take your handgun into your "strong" (trigger-finger) hand, and grip it how you usually do. Take note of how hard you are squeezing. Do you think your hand would ever get tired? Perhaps you're gripping too hard. Do you think it would be easy to pull the gun out of your hand? Perhaps you're gripping too softly.

Note how the hands support each other almost perfectly to form a rock-solid grip.

Remember this: Your grip on the handgun should be about as firm as that of a solid hand-shake. If you're not sure what that means, let me phrase it like this: You should grip your handgun with as much pressure as you would grip a hammer to drive a normal sized nail into a piece of wood.

If you grip too hard, the gun will shake badly, and it will be difficult to press the trigger smoothly. If you grip too weakly, you will have to re-adjust your grip after each shot or two, as the gun will have a tendency to 'climb' out of your hand due to the recoil. Too light a grip will also cause feeding problems in automatics: the slide can only 'cycle' if the frame of the gun remains relatively stationary, and too light a grip will not provide the necessary stability to make this happen. If your gun fails to load a full casing into the chamber, or "stove-pipes" empty cases, this may be the problem-try gripping the gun more firmly.

Practice gripping with the 'firm handshake' strength with one and two hands. Also remember that the stronger your ability to grip is, the better off you

Take special note of how the palms and thumbs lock together, and how the weak-hand thumb is being used to add additional support to the frame of the handgun.

will be, so it may be worth your while to practice grip exercises while driving and on your spare time. Get a spring-loaded grip builder, or wad up the daily newspaper in one hand before throwing them out.

Important: For a two-handed grip, you should grip a bit harder with your weak hand than with your strong (trigger finger) hand. Think of it like this: if both hands together are applying 100% of the grip force on your handgun, your weak hand should account for about 60% of that force, and your strong hand should account for the remaining 40%. This is because when you press the trigger, the harder you're gripping with your strong-hand, the more the gun will move.

What I've just described is the ideal two handed grip, but you may have to experiment to see what works best for you. Ideally, we'd all carry the guns that we can grip the most comfortably, but sometimes we have to deal with what we have.

If shooting is uncomfortable, or if the gun is recoiling excessively, your grip is the problem. Practice the proper grip, and work on wrist strength, and grip strength exercises.

Note how the weak-hand fingers lock comfortably over the strong-hand fingers.

Section 3: Trigger Control--Blast Off.

I t is important to understand that 90% of your accuracy-killing movement is going to take place DURING the trigger press, so this is crucial. The more rock-solid your grip is, the easier it's going to be to master your trigger press, and the smoother and more intentional your trigger press, the less perfect your grip has to be. Master both the grip and the press, and you will have Olympic teams calling you, begging you to come shoot for them.

Let me deviate and explain why I'm saying "trigger press" instead of "trigger pull". I think it's important, because we're all taught that you pull the trigger of a gun to make it go off. Here's the problem: We also pull stuck doors open. We PULL teeth out. We PULL ourselves up icy slopes with ropes. Such a brute action should never be used to describe what needs to take place in regards to your trigger when trying to perform an accurate shot.

Instead, we say that you must PRESS your trigger. While you can press hard on things, press generally describes a much more controlled action, as if you're applying the exact amount of force needed to make the gun go 'boom', and no more. You're not pulling or pushing your trigger- you're pressing it.

One of the most common problems that people have is that they 'flinch' the trigger. A flinch describes any action other than a smooth, fluid like trigger press. A flinch can be done unconsciously as your body's reaction to the expected recoil, or in a conscious effort to make the gun go bang during the exact second that your sights are on your target. Both of these need to STOP in order to boost your accuracy, and I will talk about how to eliminate flinching altogether in section four of this report- is can be done, quite easily. First however, you must learn the proper way to press the trigger of your gun. Remember: It all begins with the perfect grip, so make sure that you've established the principals from section two.

Learn the Stages: Next, you must master the 'stages' of your trigger. You need to know what is 'slack' in your trigger- this is the first stage. Then at some point during the press, the trigger will stiffen slightly- this is stage two. At this point, any more pressure will cause your gun to fire. How will you learn these stages? The answer is 'Dry fire'. Contrary to popular belief, dry most certainly does not hurt the firing pin or mechanism in 99% of modern guns. So ensure that your gun is empty, and dry-fire it until you are certain that you know these two stages (you'll learn more about how to dry fire in the next section).

Remember! Smooth is fast. Practice FORM, and you will become fast as form becomes trivial.

An 'accurate' trigger press will be consistent and fluid like. You can hit targets in many ways, but to group your shots closely together, logic dictates that you must do things the same each time. 2+2 always equals four. Therefore, if you hold your gun with the exact same amount of pressure, in the exact same way, and perform the exact same trigger press each time- your shots will travel the exact same path.

An accurate trigger press is accomplished with all the force being straight back- it's easy to pull slightly to one side without realizing it. If your shots are hitting directly left or right of the point of aim, you may be pushing or pulling the trigger in a direction other than straight back into the gun.

Remember- smooth is fast. Practice form, and you will naturally become fast as the form becomes trivial. Your finger can contact the trigger at either the pad of your 'finger print', or if it's too stiff (or if your finger is too long) you can use the first joint of your finger to press the trigger. Again, the important thing is that the force is applied in a perfect line toward the rear of the gun.

The perfect trigger press is as follows: With a solid grip, remove your finger from the frame of the gun and slowly bring it down to contact the trigger. I'm going to assume that your gun is in 'ready to fire' mode, and that you've decided that you do indeed want to fire a shot.

With your finger on the trigger, stare at your front sight. Your target will be somewhat blurry in the back-ground as you focus (with both eyes open) on your front sight. Your front sight will tremble slightly against the image of your target, as you focus on it. A tiny tremble or wobble is tolerable, as these wobbles are barely a quarter of a degree off axis, and will only change your point of impact by an inch per ten yards, max.

Now, smoothly press your trigger to stage two, and pause. Did your front sight wobble excessively during the press? It shouldn't wobble any more than normal. The most likely scenario is that the pressing of the trigger torques the handgun toward your weak-hand. This is because you are pressing the trigger with more force than you are gripping the gun with. Simply increase your grip force on the handgun, or if you must, begin building your grip by exercising as mentioned in section two.

Once you have stage one mastered, proceed through stage two and dry-fire your pistol. When the hammer (internal or external) fell and you heard the

An accurate trigger press is accomplished with all the force being straight back; it's easy to pull to one side without realizing it.

"click!", did you notice your front sight wobble, or jerk to the left or right at all? If so, your shot would have been anywhere from 6 to 26 inches off target. Remember- it only take a fraction of an inch's flinch to throw a shot WAY off target. Practice your trigger press until there is no movement in your front sight.

This carries us perfectly into section four.

■

Section 4: Practice to Perfection.

The key to improving your handgun accuracy is simple, and requires that you fire ZERO live rounds of ammunition. It's a little trick that I like to call... dry fire practice. Using the principals outlined above regarding grip and trigger control- even for just ten minutes before you go to sleep tonight- you will improve your ability to hit well with your handgun. Dry-Fire practice before you sleep every night for five or ten minutes for a month, and you will become a whole new shooter.

Now, you must understand one thing: dry firing most modern pistols does not hurt them. If you shoot a GLOCK, a '1911', a Kel-Tec, a Walther, a Ruger, a Smith and Wesson... none of these are harmed by dry firing. If you are unsure about your gun, you may ask someone at a gun store, or try going to google and searching for your model plus the words 'dry fire safe?', or joining one of the many fire-arm related online forums, and asking the people there.

So... what is dry fire practice? To dry-fire, is to go through the motions of 'regular' 'live-fire' practice, except you don't put any ammunition into your gun. For a double-action revolver or automatic, you just keep pulling the trigger on an empty chamber. For a single-action revolver or automatic, you just cock the hammer and squeeze, and for a GLOCK or other 'striker fire' type design, just cycle the action after every dry-fire.

During your dry fire sessions, focus on your front sight. Learn to keep your sight picture relatively clear while still focusing on the front sight, with both eyes open. This will allow you to keep your front sight on target, while eliminating as much 'wobble' as possible.

After your trigger press, focus on keeping the trigger pulled for a split-second; long enough to register that you've pulled your trigger and caused a 'shot', and that your front sight is still on target. The goal here is to reinforce the proper follow-through. The wrong way would be to instantly let go of your gun with your weak hand as you reach to cock the gun the instant the hammer falls. This will reinforce all the bad movements.

Ideally, you should stand in front of a safe back-stop when you dry fire practice- just in case.

Follow through both stages of the fire sequence, exactly how you would if you were actually shooting. The obvious goals are two get used to following through with your shot while maintaining your solid grip, and of course executing a perfect, smooth trigger press.

The 'secret advantage' of this, is that you are training your subconscious to NOT anticipate the recoil of your handgun.

If the only times you ever press your trigger, you feel a sharp jerk and an incredibly loud noise, you will develop a physical reaction... I almost guarantee it. However, if more often than not a press of a trigger results in nothing but a 'click', and with you focusing sharply on your front sight, your body and mind will forget all about the recoil and the BANG. This may not seem like a huge advantage, but if you do five or ten minutes of dry fire practice each night, the degree of advantage of this 'conditioning' will become apparent- even after just one night. Some pros say that you should be dry firing 100 times for every

Practice Makes Perfect- And now you don't even need to fire a shot!

live-shot you fire. This should make sense, now that we've talked about the conditioning aspect of dry fire practice.

If you want to put yourself to a test, try balancing something on top of your gun as you dry fire. I remember the first time that I set an empty casing on top of my GLOCK, it fell long before I ever got to stage two of the trigger press.

No wonder I was shooting poorly! Now, I am able to balance a penny on my front sight without having it fall off.

Practice your grip and trigger press for ten minutes, and then go to the range and run a few magazines through your pistol, or a few speed loaders through your revolver. You will be amazed at how drastically your accuracy improves.

Do this a few times per week, and in two month's time, you will be shooting at a level that you may never have thought possible. Best of all, this control and skill will translate to ALL forms of shooting, whether you're shooting while moving (to avoid getting shot), shooting one handed, or shooting at longer ranges.

A Note About Mental Conditioning

In the same way that Ivan Pavlov discovered that you could "teach" dogs to drool in anticipation of having their food delivered, shooting handguns "teaches" your brain to anticipate the recoil. Without even realizing that it's happening, you will begin to flinch when the hammer falls- destroying your ability to shoot highly accurately.

'Classical Conditioning' works both ways, though- you can also "teach" your brain to forget the flinch through dry fire practice.

The mind games don't stop there, either! You can use similar methods to 'program' your mind to react to all sorts of things, such as 'moving off the x' while drawing, and to clear your handgun in the event of a jam or misfire.

■

Conclusion: This is just the tip of the iceberg...

What you've just read WILL boost your handgun accuracy, and I hope you put these principals into practice today.

"Thank you, Armed American."

At the United States Concealed Carry Association, we believe strongly in the importance of not only being armed, but being effectively armed. We believe that if you are going to go armed, you owe it to yourself and to everyone you will come in contact with to be proficient with your weapon, and alert in your mind.

That is why we set out every day to build our website, our members-only forum, our magazine, and our books and special reports even stronger. We recognize that we are indeed the Ultimate Resource for the Armed Citizen.

Yes, we've got thousands of life-saving articles containing tips and tricks on our website. Yes, we've got over 200,000 posts on our members-only forum from dedicated members. Yes, we have built our magazine so strong that it's hailed as the most relevant and energetic gun-related magazine in the world. And yes, our products, including the one that this report was inspired by (107+ Handgun Accuracy Secrets), have helped our members lead happier and safer lives.

But we also recognize that part of being an armed citizen is that there is ALWAYS room for improvement, and the second you stop charging forward is the second you start slipping backward.

If you take the responsibility of going armed as seriously as we do, I hope you'll consider becoming a member of the United States Concealed Carry Association, alongside the 31,000+ people who have done so before you.

As a member of the USCCA, you will:

- Support and defend your right to self-defense.

- Make new friends with like-minded folks on our private forum.

- Join the TENS of THOUSANDS of Americans who are already members.

- Save time and money with our concealed carry gun and gear reviews.

- Enjoy your own subscription to Concealed Carry Magazine.

- Learn the latest in training & self-defense techniques.

- Enjoy peace-of-mind knowing you're properly prepared.

- Have the chance to review new and exciting products as part of our 'Product Testing Program'.

- Have access to exclusive member 'video tips' online.

- Hear thrilling accounts of armed citizens using their carry guns to save innocent lives.

- Enjoy unlimited access to handy tools, such as our "Carry Instructor Locator" and "Reciprocity Map".

- Become an eclusive member of our online community, home to thousands of armed Americans.

"Welcome Home, Armed Citizen."

(read on... we've got something special in mind for you!)

If you are as passionate as we are about our God-Given right to self-defense and our constitutionally protected right to keep and bear arms, I hope you'll click the "Learn More" link below this paragraph to see the offer that we have prepared for you.

"The Deal of the Century."

For the same price as a yearly membership, we want to make you a member, and also GIVE you the full book that inspired the report that you just read. That's right, we want to give you a copy of 107+ Handgun Accuracy Secrets just for becoming a member of the USCCA today.

We have sold thousands of copies of this book for $47, but it's yours, along with the countless other benefits that you'll get from your membership to the USCCA.

Get the details on how you can get your copy of 107+ Handgun Accuracy Secrets absolutely free when you become the newest member of the USCCA.

"The Thousands of archived articles are an AMAZING resource!"

I just had to write to commend you for the great service that you provide all of us members. The thousands of archived articles are an amazing resource! They highlight and explain defense methods, discuss a wide variety of new or emerging equipment, and some even give us a good laugh along with imparting knowledge.

The video clips that are included with the on-line newsletter are always something to look forward to. Some are serious, some are humorous, some are both, all are informative. As a member, the USCCA magazine we receive keeps us informed while away from the computer. Of equal importance, it allows us to easily share important information with friends and other people we know.

I especially like the magazine section that reports instances of folks providing for their own personal safety and those of others through the use of a personal firearm. We do not find that kind of important, positive reporting in any of the large public media. Your forum and the many other areas in your website continue to keep us enlightened!

Terje A. L. Bolef

St. Louis , Missouri

"Helped me decide WHAT to carry, and HOW to carry it."

"The USCCA has helped me immensely in deciding what to carry and how to carry it. I can't say enough about the USCCA and CC Magazine. "

Scott Smart

Hastings, MN

■

Made in the USA
San Bernardino, CA
11 April 2014